SEEDS TO GROW SUCCESS:

FOUNDATIONAL TOOLS FOR THE ROOKIE REAL ESTATE AGENT TO BUILD A PROFITABLE BUSINESS

RAMELIA

FIRST EDITION

ISBN: 978 – 0 – 6151 – 8402 – 9

This publication is designed to provide accurate and authoritative information in regard to the subject matter covered. It is sold with the understanding that the publisher is not engaged in rendering legal, financial or accounting service. If legal advice or other expert assistance is required, the services of a competent professional should be sought.

"Success is to be measured not so much by the position that one has reached in life as by the obstacles which he has overcome while trying to succeed."

~Booker T. Washington

Acknowledgements

Thank you to . . .

Thank you, my God and Father, for the inspiration and the courage to become who I was designed to be, authentically and with no apologies;

Dad and Mom, for being the channels, protectors and developers of the gift of my life;

Uncle Poochie and Aunt Sharon, for providing me with the serene thinking space to begin this journey;

My Mom, who always listens to my "latest and greatest" far-fetched ideas and lets me know I can accomplish anything I set my mind to;

Mahalia (Mia Boo), Tania (Nana), and Myles...Always remember that the dream farthest from your reach is the thing to reach for;

My coaches, Andrew Morrison, Christy Geiger, and Wes Miller; you may not know it, but you helped me make it over the hump...keep transforming lives;

All my sister girlfriends for believing in me and encouraging me;

My sisters for always supporting my new endeavors;

My Favorite brother for being a dedicated, repeat real estate client who taught me that "one cannot discover new oceans until one has the courage to lose sight of the shore"~ unknown;

The contributors of expert knowledge that helped create this manuscript: LaVerne Young, Nina Chen, Michael Dipasquale, Bertina Power and Janice Corley-Blaney; and

Last but not least, BJ, for needing to go out for a walk when I didn't think I needed a break, for being silently supportive, and for warming my toes under the desk.

TABLE OF CONTENTS

FOREWORD

This project was truly a labor of love and definitely an "oops" child that I had no idea was on the way. I am passionate about sharing wisdom and guidance with people searching for direction. Compensation and fulfillment in my life come from knowing that I have helped someone do better or be better in their life.

INTRODUCTION

"There is a difference between interest and commitment; when you are interested in something, you do it only when it is convenient, when you are committed to something you accept no excuses, only results."

–Mark McCabe

This book was written for those who are committed to building a thriving real estate sales business that helps the people in their community or target market make informed and educated real estate decisions. It is especially written for new licensees who are looking to shorten their learning curve and jump-start their business. This book will bathe you in knowledge, motivation and foundational tools for growing a successful real estate sales business. Growing a business, at the very root level, is about using tools to implement systems that generate a desired and profitable end result. "Seeds to Grow Success" expresses this idea and uses its chapter titles to parallel it to the process of a farmer cultivating the land to produce a harvest. In this way, the strategies are communicated in a unique, metaphoric and illustrative fashion that is engaging and thought-provoking.

This manuscript was designed to be a short, easy read, with creative marketing plans and practical activities that can be implemented in your business today. It is a book written by a real estate agent for real estate agents. I began my real estate career only a short five years ago; therefore, I am still intimately familiar with the perils and challenges of changing industries to enter the world of real estate entrepreneurs. I was very fortunate to begin my career with a company that was dedicated to the training and development of its agents. It was my experience that cooperative agents on my transactions always assumed I was a veteran agent, because of the expertise and knowledge I exhibited as a direct result of sales coaching, training and development. Use this book as a tool to get you started down the pathway to a successful, bountiful real estate sales harvest.

CHAPTER 1

FROM ROOKIE AGENT TO SUCCESSFUL AGENT: PERSISTENT AS A WEED

"Let us not become weary in doing good, for at the proper time we will reap a harvest if we do not give up." – Galatians 6:9

"Most of the important things in the world have been accomplished by people who have kept on trying when there seemed to be no hope at all." – Dale Carnegie

I spent the first six months of my real estate career wondering if I had made the right choice. The major challenge of my first full year in the business came from being a rookie agent. It was a challenge to feel confident about calling myself a real estate agent when I had not yet sold a single property. Even worse, I had not yet personally become a property owner, at that time. Most of the sellers I encountered were looking for past experience in their agent, but I couldn't get that experience if no one gave me a chance. Also, it took a while to gain confidence and to learn how to effectively handle the "salesperson resistance" that buyers typically display.

After three months and no deals, my hope was slowly fading, and I began to think that a real estate sales career was not for me. The statistics said I needed to have at least one written contract in the first three months or most likely I was not cut out for this business. At the beginning of Month 5, I felt that I needed to change companies. But I realized that I needed to first be success-ful where I had begun, before uprooting and starting all over again. In the meantime, real life did not cease to exist, and my savings were running out. By the time the six-month mark rolled around, I was looking for a "real job."

I was seven months into my career before I pended my first deal. Ironically, within that single week, I pended three deals for different clients. That summer, I secured my first three listings within a two-week time frame, and I ended my first full year in the business with $2.1 million in sales volume. The following year I appeared on the cover of the national "Realtor Magazine" in the "30 under 30" feature article that profiles 30 Realtors under the age of 30, from across the nation, poised for success in the real estate industry.

Group coaching, sales resistance training, practicing scripts, consistent open houses, and choosing a neighborhood on which I could become an expert were some of the things that finally got me off the sidelines and into the game.

The other underlying force at work was my intense desire to succeed. I began to feel that I had little or no time left in which to make this career work. Napoleon Hill tells a parable that I will paraphrase by saying, "When you want something as much as you would want a breath of air if your head were submerged in a bucket of water, then you will have success." Parallel to that thought, Hill also wrote, "Every person who wins in any undertaking must be willing to burn his ships and cut all sources of retreat. Only by doing so can one be sure of maintaining that state of mind known as a burning desire to win, essential to success." In embarking upon a career in real estate sales, you have to let go of any back-door exit strategy brewing in your mind. With no way of escape, and with focused energies and effort, it will work out for your good.

Here are six strategies to help you get through the rough spots that you will encounter in your real estate sales career and/or in life:

1.   **Remember the dream.** Now would be a good time to review your goals. There is a prize to be won in reaching your goals. Renew the vision in your mind; picture yourself winning the prize. Beginning with the end in mind gives you the desire to keep striving to reach your goals.

2.   **Have faith in your ability to succeed.** Remember where you came from and past successes in your life and career. Remembering that you have overcome great obstacles in the past gives you renewed hope in your ability. Speak daily affirmations about your ability to overcome and to achieve greatness in spite of the odds. Believe that failure is not an option, and that the present hardship will be a distant memory in the near future.

3.   **Re-evaluate the plan**. Determine what is working for your business and what is not providing

any results. Have the courage to discard any system that is a liability instead of an asset to your business. Increase the usage of systems and activities that enhance productivity in your business. Plans are created with the knowledge base that you have at the time they are implemented. As you grow in knowledge, don't be afraid to revise the original plan for greater efficiency.

4.   **Perpetual growth.** What activity do you undertake in your business that requires consistent effort that you have not been diligent about making? Review your schedule and make sure that those activities are being accomplished. Reward yourself for seven days' worth of consistency in the task.

5.   **Learn the lesson.** What is this setback trying to teach me? If you don't learn the lesson now, this challenge will come back around again. Instead of playing the "blame game," discover the lesson and move on.

6.   **Accountability is key.** Coaching sessions, group or individual, can help you develop prob-

able solutions to your problem. You will then
be held accountable for making a decision that
will turn it around. Your coach will see to it
that you get over the hump and take action to
cause change in your situation.

So when times get rough in your real estate career ~
and they will ~ just keep putting one foot in front of the
other, even though it feels like you are going nowhere. The
law of physics says of momentum that objects in motion
stay in motion, while objects at rest stay at rest. The most
important thing is to get moving, even if you are moving
slowly.

The story of the Moso Bamboo tree creates a visual
for how perseverance and pushing through the hard times
can reward you in the end. The Moso Bamboo tree seed-
ling is planted, watered and exposed to sunlight for *five years*
before any evidence of its existence breaks through the
ground. There is no reward for the caretaker of this tree for
many years. But if he neglects to render the proper care
and nourishment in those critical years, there will be no
growth of the tree in the end. At the appropriate time
however, the diligent efforts of the caretaker during the

long years of no reward and no harvest, will lead to great victory. The crucial key here is to keep working hard, even though you do not see results instantaneously. After its inevitable breakthrough, this tree grows about 2½ feet per day, until six weeks later it is 90 feet closer to the sky. (Some say you can even hear it growing!) How is this possible? During those five seemingly dormant years, great growth and progress is taking place underneath the surface. The Moso Bamboo tree spends its first five years of life developing a strong root system that will support its eventual enormous growth. These roots have taken the time to find nourishing resources and anchored stability, knowing the greatness that it has been created to exhibit. Patiently persisting in the building of its foundation is essential to its ability to sustain such colossal growth in such a short amount of time. Time spent prospecting, networking, sitting open houses, practicing scripts, showing property and contacting For Sale by Owners (FSBOs) may at first seem like thankless, fruitless labor, but if you stay the course, inevitable success will break forth in your business at the appropriate time. When your foundational efforts have grown to the point of being able to nourish and support success, you will possess it.

.

CHAPTER 2

GOAL-SETTING:
DESIGNING YOUR LANDSCAPE

"For I know where I came from and where I am going . . ."
– Jesus in John 8:14

"A rudderless ship and a purposeless person are eventually stranded on desert sand." – Napoleon Hill

Goal-setting is a paramount key to success. It is said that one who fails to plan also plans to fail. Goals are set for us, from the time we are conceived. After conception, a child is planned to be birthed in 9-10 months. Our parents' goal and hope is that we walk by our first birthday. We are expected to be potty trained by age 3. We are expected to start traditional schooling by age 5 or 6. We then have a goal to complete elementary education by age 13 or 14, and secondary education by age 18 or 19. From there, in typical situations, our goal-setting and life-planning is placed in our hands.

After graduating from college, I realized that there were no longer parentally or governmentally imposed goals for me to reach. It was now all up to me. Where did I want to go? What did I want to do? Where did I want to be? What did I want to become? It was then that I also pondered family goals. Who would I marry? How many children, if any, would I bear? Existing outside of my previous goal-imposed world was a scary place to be. The absence of goals meant no direction, no focus, no place to belong, no structure, no reason to strive, no reason to press on.

Once I began to take control and set goals, there was more order and structure to my life. But, later I realized that I had set my goals far beneath my level of potential. My major life goal, after completing college, was to be self-sufficient: a homeowner, self-employed and free of my parents' household. In June of 2004, this life goal reached fruition. I had become a condominium owner, was self-employed as a real estate consultant, and appeared that month on the cover of the national "Realtor" magazine as one of the nation's "30 under 30" real estate executives to watch. I had achieved greatness ~ my definition of greatness, that is. And then it happened; the downward spiral began. I asked myself so many times how I could fall so hard from the mountaintop. After countless months of reflection, meditation and journaling, I realized that part of my ensuing decline stemmed from the fact that I had not given myself further direction. I had reached the pinnacle of success, according to my definition. My psyche was then asking the question: *Now what? Where do we go from here?* But there was no response, only the echoing sound of the question. I believe that my sights were set too low for the potential of greatness inside me. My mistake was not quickly creating another life goal after accomplishing the previous one.

Goals, dreams and visions are important for every area of our lives. Below is a list of goal-setting questions and thoughts you can ponder as you begin to establish and write down goals for your life and business.

1.   **Life fulfillment goals:** What is your life's major purpose and how is it fulfilled in your daily life? Write your obituary. What do you want it to

say? How do you want to be remembered? Create some goals that will allow you to live the story you just wrote.

2.   <u>**Health/Fitness goals:**</u> Do I need to lose excess weight? Do I need to establish a weekly exercise routine? Can I make it a goal to get off of a medication I've been prescribed by enacting some natural method of healing like losing weight, changing my eating habits or beginning an exercise program?

3.   <u>**Family goals:**</u> Do we spend enough quality time together? Can I make it a goal to have game night 3 times per month, family dinner time once per week, or date night 3 times per month with my significant other?

4.   <u>**Spiritual goals:**</u> Have I set aside time for daily meditation/prayer? Do I attend worship/fellowship services on a regular basis? Can I carve out space in my schedule to volunteer or give of my time to others, in some way?

5.　　**Mental exercise:** When you cease to learn, you cease to grow. Do I read regularly that I might grow? Make it a goal to take a weekend class that focuses on a hobby or other subject of interest you might enjoy learning. Consider taking a class to learn another language.

6.　　**Personal financial goals:** Make a goal to rid yourself of credit-card debt within a predetermined number of months. Plan to build your savings account to a specified dollar amount. How much will you set aside from each commission check to deposit in investment vehicles? Do you have an emergency fund that can cover 3-6 months of living expenses?

7.　　**Professional goals:** Forecast your gross annual income for the year. Set a goal to increase the number of prospects in your marketing database. Quarterly income goals can help you determine how many prospects you need to come in contact with, in order to reach your goals.

How many listing appointments do you need to go on in a month to achieve your target number of listings taken for the quarter? When you conduct open houses, keep a running tally of how many guests walk through the home versus how many you actually work with as clients. This ratio determines your client conversion ratio. Set a goal to increase your conversion percentage. Consider increasing the average dollar value of your transactions. Analyze the positive return on investment for advertising dollars spent. Make a plan to increase the return on your advertising dollars. Endeavor to increase the number of your referral-generated leads by a certain percentage.

Goals cause you to strive and put forth focused effort to reach a predetermined point. Lewis Carroll said, "If you don't know where you're going, any road will get you there." In <u>The One-Minute Manager</u>, Ken Blanchard put it like this: "How long would [you] want to bowl if there were no pins? ...Who would watch football if there were no goals to shoot at or any way to score? ...The number one motivator of people is feedback on results."

Having goals gives you a measure of success. When I started endurance running, I could have progressed through my training program and run 30 miles without thinking it a major accomplishment. But because I set a goal at the beginning to run the Chicago Marathon, a 26.2-mile race, it was a major accomplishment ~ not so much because of the number of miles but because I had set out to reach a goal and I had achieved it. Since I knew the date of the race, a timeline could be established for my training. My running coach prepared a weekly workout schedule, figuring backwards from the goal...Race Day.

It is much the same in business. Knowing your ultimate goal or destination, you are able to plan the smaller journeys along the way that will get you there. Effective goal-setting requires that each goal be broken down into quarterly, monthly, weekly, then daily actionable steps. Make sure these activities are very specific and measurable. For example, if my actionable step was to run 50 total miles during my first month of training, that leaves too much room for debate and procrastination. My actionable steps need to be much more precise. In this instance, my steps should be defined as running 2 miles a day, 4 days per week, and on the 4 consecutive Saturdays of the month run 2, 3, 4 and 5 miles, respectively. These activities are well-defined and easily measurable.

Now, let's say you set a goal to increase the number of people in your marketing database. In order to make this goal specific and measurable, determine how many additional people you would like to add in a defined space of time. Project the number of social functions you need to attend, marketing activities you need to conduct, and/or phone calls you need to make in order to achieve that number of people. Your goal might look like this:

- Add 50 people to the marketing database in the next 30 days.
    - o Attend 2 networking groups per week for the next month. This will generate 5 names from each networking group to add to the database.
    - o Call 15 people per week for the next 4 weeks from the current database and ask who they know that is currently interested in buying or selling property. From each set of 15 people

called, 3 names will be generated to add to the database.

Celebrate the small successes on the way to your ultimate goal. It is the progressive journey through small victories that leads us to our ultimate triumph. Each small success offers the hope of greater achievement. Enjoy the process because your final destination is only a place of temporary rest before going after your next goal.

Keeping your eyes focused on your goal and not becoming distracted from its achievement is another key to successful goal-setting. Daily affirmations are a way to keep your goals at the forefront of your mind. The Bible says, "Write the vision and make it plain . . .," Habakkuk 2:2. It also states that "The tongue has the power of life and death . . .," Proverbs 18:21. Therefore, envision your success and what you want to achieve. Then write the vision by formulating your dreams into written goals, and speak daily affirmations according to your written goals. ". . . For out of the overflow of the heart the mouth speaks," Luke 6:45. What you speak daily will become engrained in your heart as your truth and eventually your reality. Create your own set of daily affirmations that emanate from your goals.

Following are examples of some of my personal affirmations:

1. My eyes are focused on my goals; I will not be sidetracked.

2. I have a good future and prosperous business ahead of me; no obstacle is able to hinder me.

3. Stone by stone, step by step, day by day, this business is taking shape, and that which was not is now becoming.

4. My days are organized and scheduled; thereby I am efficient and productive with my time.

5. There is a need for the services I provide; as they are marketed, there is an overflow of customers and prospects waiting to be serviced.

6. I have been chosen to bless people with the services of this business. I serve with joy and am rewarded with fulfillment and contentment.

7. I am peaceful and patient with the employees, vendors, clients, sponsors and partners of this business.

8. I am confident and *act* in spite of any fears that try to immobilize me.

9. Momentum . . . objects in motion stay in motion, objects at rest stay at rest. I will keep moving and stay productive.

10. My business produces financial reward that allows me to be debt-free and financially stable, with the ability to give freely to others.

Without effective goal-setting, you expect nothing of yourself and aim at nothing . . . hitting the target every time.

CHAPTER 3

TIME MANAGEMENT:
PLANNING FOR THE HARVEST

"To everything there is a time and purpose under heaven."
Ecclesiastes 3:1

"...Time... [It is] mine to develop, mine to utilize and mine to manage.
The reverse is true as well – [it is] mine to waste." – David Ivey

Effective time management is the second fundamental building block of success. Without proper time management skills, your life is steered as a reactive instead of proactive vessel. You are so busy putting out fires and responding to others' needs that you look up at sunset to realize that your day has been extremely unproductive. How did a whole day go by without your accomplishing or working towards a single task on your To-Do list? The answer lies in your reactive behavior. You start your day waiting for the phone to ring so that you can have your marching orders for the day. Jim Rohn puts it like this, "Either you run the day or the day runs you." Alternatively, when you engage proactive measures to manage your time, you will make a powerful and profitable paradigm shift in your business.

Effective time management skills allow you to structure your day toward a productive end. When we have many scheduled activities, our day is, in effect, managed by time. We know where we should be at a certain time and how much time we have allotted to get there. We know what appointments we have scheduled, as far as two weeks or more in advance, and we don't run the risk of double booking meetings.   For many of us who have gone from a "punch the clock" type of employment to a self-employed, "my time is my own" status, we quickly realize why that order and structure were necessary for our previous employer to run a profitable and productive business. Yet we respect our former boss and company more than we respect our new boss…ourselves! We would not dare take a nap on the boss's time. We dare not leave the office and drive our sister, cousin, mother, friend shopping on the boss's time. We dare not take a four-hour lunch break that included grocery shopping, car oil change, hair appointment and massage. There is nothing wrong with including these activities in our schedule because they are necessary. But we must become more deliberate and intentional about when and how we spend our time. "We must give our business the same respect we gave our last boss," says Janice Corley-Blaney of Sudler Sotheby's International Realty in Chicago.

Time is one of the most precious gifts that God has given us, but we don't value it as such. Napoleon Hill demonstrated this thought by writing, "Hurry, the sand in your hourglass is running lower every second, and the glass can not be refilled." When someone lies on their deathbed, the desire most expressed is the desire for more time. When one knows that the end of their life is near, they tend to do more with less, valuing each precious moment spent with loved ones. I often hear people say, "I tried to do this or that but I ran out of time." You cannot run out of time, because the same 24 hours is given to each of us every day that we have life. It would be more appropriate to say, "I mismanaged the time I had to spend."

Effective time management is a daily, weekly and monthly task. Once you have set goals and objectives, the time management schedule is fairly easy to create. Using your monthly goals, create a list of the activities necessary to help you reach those goals. Using a daily/weekly calendar with one-hour time slots, schedule each activity in one-to-three-hour time blocks. In scheduling your activities, consider yourself; schedule challenging activities when you are invigorated and mentally fresh. The activities that are most enjoyable to you can be scheduled when your energy may be relatively low. Your calendar should include client appointments, personal activities, individual and/or group coaching appointments, open houses, administrative activities, family time, networking events, office meetings, day(s) off, etc.

Time scheduling serves to structure your time so that you can operate like the business that you are. Without a structured format for the day, we tend to do what we feel like doing, when we feel like doing it. A functional, profitable business should not be subjected to your emotional rollercoaster ride. Feelings are fickle and thus have no place in a stable, productive business operation. Start establishing structure by setting office hours during which you are available to clients and to work on your business. When agents are asked by clients when they can be reached,

I often hear them say they are available "24/7." No one should have a schedule that does not leave room for rest and renewal; such a relentless schedule will undoubtedly lead to burnout. Agents subconsciously believe that being constantly "on-call" is part of the real estate agent's job description. I have known agents who are not even able to go to the bathroom without taking their phone into the stall with them. When you communicate your business structure upfront, such as days off, office hours and time for returning voicemails, clients respect it. Your established structure and systems communicate the message that you are organized and proficient at your trade. If God could make the world in six days and desire rest on the seventh, to take a step back and reflect on what was accomplished, then you should also implement this in your time scheduling. "It's useless to rise early and go to bed late, and work your worried fingers to the bone. Don't you know He enjoys giving rest to those he loves?" ~Psalm 127:2

Time management also serves to keep us on track toward our goals. The time management schedule becomes a timeline for completion of our activities. This structure creates a self-imposed urgency to accomplish the work set before you. This moves you from mental chaos to well-defined order. For those who have a hard time resisting time-stealers, this creates a structure that leaves very little opportunity for time-wasters to creep in. Although you should schedule all activities, make sure that you remain flexible, as unscheduled fires do occasionally need to be attended to. Following are some tips to keep you on-time and on schedule.

Top Ten Time-Management Tips for Real Estate Agents:

1. When you meet with buyers, let them know how long you have allotted for their appointment to look at the houses you have scheduled for that day. This will help you make it to your next appointment or activity on time. Make sure that you have scheduled enough time for the client to look and ponder without feeling rushed.

2. Plan to arrive 15 minutes before an appointment, in case there is traffic or minimal parking available.

3. Include traveling time between showings and appointments in your schedule.

4.   Track and analyze your time weekly to deter-
       mine how much of your time is productive
       (spent with clients) versus nonproductive (ad-
       ministrative activities, seminars, etc.) Set goals
       to increase your productive hours as necessary.

5.   Review tomorrow's activities today; make sure
       that you are prepared for upcoming client ap-
       pointments and presentations.

6.   If you procrastinate on making prospecting
       phone calls, schedule your time block of calls
       with an accountability partner, to make sure
       that prospecting sessions happen. It is said that
       it takes 21 days to form a habit. Schedule a
       month's worth of these sessions with your part-
       ner, until you develop the habit of prospecting.

7.   If you do your most challenging activity every
       day of the week it is scheduled, i.e. prospecting
       phone calls, reward yourself!

8.   During your time-blocked activities, do not take
       phone calls or accept any other interruptions.
       (This includes answering the cell phone during
       client appointments; this communicates to the
       client that their transaction is not as important

as your next deal.) If you work in a brokerage and are prospecting, display a sign on your desk that says "Prospecting ~ Do Not Disturb."

9. Use daily "To Do" lists for phone calls that need to be made/returned or other random activities that need to be done. Use empty time slots in your schedule to accomplish these tasks. At the end of your workday, create a "To Do" list for the following day that includes the items on today's list that were not completed.

10. Your voicemail message that callers hear should remind callers of your office hours and of the two time-blocked timeframes that you have scheduled for returning phone calls and messages; generally speaking, you should have a morning and late afternoon slot for returning messages.

CHAPTER 4

FIND YOUR NICHE:
PLANT ONE CROP AT A TIME

"Let every man wherein he is called, therein abide with God."
1 Corinthians 7:24

"Fit thyself into the environment that thou findest on earth."
– Marcus Aurelius

Some time ago, I read a rhyme in a church bulletin that encouraged its parishioners to advertise in the bulletin by saying something like, "If you have a thing to sell and go and whisper it in a well, you are not apt to make as many dollars as if you were to climb up in a tree and holler." Marketing your services is a necessary component of the strategy to run a profitable business. Marketing programs and systems come in many forms. There is referral marketing, direct mail marketing, media advertising, geographic farming and many others to choose from. Which one is the best way to market your services?

I pondered the same question for a long time when I entered the real estate industry. In the end, the answer to my question was this: they are all good, income-producing methods. The key is to choose the one that is right for you, and to work it consistently. Factors to consider are cost, effectiveness and time for implementation. Take a look at your strengths and weaknesses, and choose a system that complements your strengths. Once you choose a system, track its productivity in your business, if it does not produce the results you anticipated, try a different method. As a rookie agent, you generally have more time than money to spend. In this case, a referral marketing program or open house and floor-time lead generation method works best to start to build your clientele base. If you have a marketing budget and prefer an indirect approach to marketing, direct-mail marketing or media advertising may work better for you. Regardless of the type of marketing system you select, you can magnify its effectiveness by choosing a marketing niche to target. When you choose a target market, you become an expert on the needs and experiences of the people in that niche, and thus become invaluable to the members of the niche group.

Your niche can be formed socially or geographically. Socially, the niche can be people of a particular profession or demographic group. The following are examples of social markets that you can target to offer your services: teachers, police officers, doctors, lawyers, pet lovers, retirees, widows, divorcees, seniors, recent college graduates, single parents, people with wounded credit, first-time homebuyers, vacation home seekers, luxury home buyers (homes priced over $500,000), pastors, self-employed individuals, investors, etc. When you provide specialized customer service to your target market, you set your services apart from the services of the many generalist agents in the industry. Researching property title concerns, specialized mortgage products, legitimate credit-repair programs, down-payment assistance programs, closing-cost grant programs, residential areas with desirable facilities important to the social market (i.e. dog parks, children's parks, running/biking paths, harbor with boat docks), community groups of interest (i.e. senior villages), and other resources as they relate to individuals in your niche, will make you more knowledgeable and useful as an agent to your customer base. You can also approach these specialty lenders, grant programs, attorneys, and other key people to create special discount programs, offers and coupons for your group. Then, assemble these key pieces of information that are of value to your niche to create a customized marketing package/folder to be distributed in various ways to your target market. These marketing pieces can be distributed at your real estate seminars for the niche group, or they can be offered to prospects as a "free special report" for signing up on your website. This will become your marketing collateral, to be implemented in any marketing or advertising campaigns you run. You are branding yourself as the real estate expert for this niche group of people, knowing that special, specific expertise gives you a major advantage.

One of the "social" niche markets I serviced as an agent was investors seeking income-producing, multi-unit property. I created partnerships with lenders that specialized in residential commercial financing, and attorneys that specialized in legal representation for this type of property. For this particular clientele, I used formulas to determine the return on investment for every property they were shown, based on their particular financial situation. Upon arriving at a property showing, in addition to the MLS listing sheet, I would provide the client with a personalized financial that detailed the estimated monthly payment amount, fixed and variable expenses, gross rent multiplier, capitalization rate, gross monthly/annual income, net monthly/annual income, net operating income, and the return on their proposed investment. I also provided varied financials for the various loan programs they were considering. Experience with this niche taught me that nothing – not location, not curb appeal, not even the condition of the interior of the units – mattered as much as the numbers. This target market was far less emotionally driven in making a purchase decision. Understanding this and other specific needs of this market helped me to offer personalized service that they could appreciate. Consequently, I was very successful in marketing to and thus serving this target market.

Geographically, you can choose to target your services to residents of a particular neighborhood, subdivision, condominium complex or other geographic area. If you choose to market geographically, it is imperative that you create a 5-, 7- or 10-year market analysis that includes details of the progression of the chosen target area from a market value perspective. Include average list price to sales price ratios, number of units sold, number of units available and average dollar value of specific property types for each year in the study. (All of this information can be researched in the MLS system.) This report should include an analysis of the changes in market value for various residential property types or condominium unit sizes, information on new commercial and residential developments, school district information, vacant land proposals, and zoning ordinances. (For extra credit, you can add recreational and dining options in the area.) This report will take time to create, but it will prove invaluable in establishing your credibility and professionalism with potential clients. Give the study a professional look and feel by branding the cover with your name, business logo and contact information. Get the study bound with spiral binding at your local printer. As mentioned above, this study can be offered to prospects at real estate seminars and open houses, or as a "free report" on your website. You will set yourself apart from agents who just search the real estate database and give clients information about property and areas for which they have no specific experience or knowledge. This extensive market analysis can also be useful at listing presentations, exhibiting your knowledge of the area and credible information you would present to prospective buyers who visit the home. In this way, you establish yourself as an "expert" on the area.

Following are five ideas to get your brain cycling around the thought of a potential niche that you might like to target with your chosen marketing and/or advertising campaigns whether you choose a social or geographic marketing plan.

1. **There's no place like home.** Your own condominium, subdivision, or neighborhood is the best place to start (provided that you have been a good neighbor.) This is a place where you are well known, if not by name then definitely by face. You can be seen shopping, walking your dog, taking your children to school, cutting the grass, going for a jog, etc. Clients like to work with people they know and trust. Face recognition and a simple "Hi, how are you today?" can go a long way toward setting up the foundation for a trustworthy relationship. Another phenomenon that I have discovered is that people like to live where real estate agents live. Because we are wise about "all things real es-

tate" in the consumer's eyes, it is sometimes helpful to mention to a buyer that you live in the particular area, condominium, or subdivision they are considering. During a listing presentation, this can also give you an advantage over your competition. Being a resident of the community, you have personal knowledge and passion for the area that an outside agent cannot compete with. As your business grows, you become the local resident expert on real estate in the area.

2. **Who do you know?** Is there a group of people within which you have lots of acquaintances or connections? These are great groups within which to establish yourself as the real estate agent of choice. I knew a real estate agent whose husband was a medical doctor. Having been with her husband through medical school and residency, she understood the intimate needs and stresses of a medical resident moving to a new town and having to find a new place to live within a few months' time. Appreciating some of the unique traits of this demographic, she targeted this market with great success, meeting the needs of this demographic in a

variety of ways. Knowing that medical residents have little time for a social life, she made it her business to find out what they liked to do socially, and then prepared a list of options available in the city, including entertainment, places of worship, gyms, etc. These resident doctors spend most of their time at the hospital. Consequently, she became well acquainted with property options and availability near the hospitals in town, knowing the importance for these clients of living in close proximity to their assigned hospital. The clients' lack of assets and work and income history created a need for special loan financing; thus, she developed partnerships with lenders that specialized in providing financing for this debt-heavy, asset-challenged group. Understanding 24-hour on-call days, she adjusted her schedule to be prepared for late evening or midnight conversations when the client had time to discuss the transaction.

3. **Do you have a passion for making people feel welcome in a new place?** Do you enjoy showing guests around town when they come to visit you? Do you warm up quickly and comfortably to people you do

not know? You might flourish with a niche in the relocation market. These agents generally service employees of large corporations. My sister's husband works for a major insurance company, and they constantly move around as he climbs the corporate ladder. When my sister investigates a new town and its culture, she begins her search online. An agent looking to service this market needs to be technologically savvy, since much of this transaction is conducted long-distance. These buyers need to see lots of properties, sometimes in as short a span as two days' time. Often, my sister and her husband will come into a new town for a single weekend and choose a neighborhood and new home, based on information provided to them by the agent. When these corporate employees come into town, your calendar needs to be cleared for the weekend; they need your full attention to help them make a huge purchase and life decision in the span of a day or two. Neighborhood tours and information on school districts, social activities and entertainment venues are always important to my sister's family, and to other buyers in this niche. The rapid, transitional nature of the relocation is much the same for sellers in this niche. Very often, sellers must leave the city before their home sells, and consequently leave the listing agent responsible for their home. You may need to coordinate lawn care, cleaning or painting services in the seller's absence. It would be to your advantage to take the classes necessary to obtain the CRS (Certified Residential Specialist) designation, to become more familiar with the skills necessary to service this market. These transactions are guaranteed sales, but be prepared to do three times the amount of paperwork needed for a normal transaction.

4. **Get in where you fit in.** The groups and associations of which you are a member can be a good place to start as well. Because you are a member of the group, you are already thought of as trustworthy among its members. Maybe you could become the real estate agent of choice for your church, promising transactions with integrity. A Mary Kay consultant could become established as the preferred real estate agent for the beauty care consultants of that company. As a board member for your con-

dominium, subdivision or block club association, you could establish yourself as the real estate specialist for the building, subdivision or block.

5. **Develop your business.** The developer market is another possible avenue. The beauty of this niche is the potential for a steady flow of buyers and property listings. One caveat regarding this relationship is that it may sometimes feel like an employer/employee relationship, after working with the same developer for an extended period of time. Depending on the developer, you may also lose the opportunity to represent sellers and buyers who are not customers of the developer. Be prepared to offer this clientele such services as pre-sale marketing programs, zoning ordinance research and permit application processing services. Partnering with a property staging company or gaining staging certification yourself could be very advantageous. Partnering with an interior design company would also prove useful to the developer while preparing the model units for showings. Creating a team of agents prepared to sit weekly open houses for buyers and brokers would be a great benefit, as well. Be

prepared to wow this niche with innovative marketing and advertising programs, to get their units under contract in record time.

In a world of generalists, especially in the real estate
industry, the most successful agents set themselves apart by
doing what others will not do or have not done. Offer
something within your real estate services that no one else
in your market offers. Target a niche for which your
competition has failed to create a specialized, targeted
approach. Decide who you want your customers to be. As
a new licensee, begin by choosing only one niche, before
targeting multiple. Take time to think about the specific
needs of the niche that you will target. What special
services can you implement in your business that would
make the process of buying or selling a home less burden-
some and more enjoyable for this niche? What services
could you offer this niche that would create one-stop
shopping for them, even if that means partnering with
another business who offers the desired service? What can
you offer that goes above and beyond the call of duty, to
completely satisfy this niche clientele? Be creative. Brain-

storm different ideas, choose a couple, and make a plan for implementing them.

CHAPTER 5

ACCOUNTABILITY:
SALES HARVEST AT STAKE

"But woe to him who is alone when he falls and has not another to lift him up." – Ecclesiastes 4:10

"No man can achieve greatness alone."
– Napoleon Hill

The concept of accountability guarantees that the foundational wisdom you have gleaned for your new career has not been gathered in vain. Accountability partners, mentors and/or coaches assure that you achieve the goals and objectives that you have established for yourself. Some person or group to hold you accountable ensures that you will be operating at maximum levels of efficiency, producing results and treating obstacles as opportunities instead of road blocks. Accountability reinforces your focus so that you do not take your eye off the goal.

Consider the purpose for and process of using wooden stakes to support plants in a garden. This is an excerpt from an article written by J.A. Young, entitled "Garden Plants at Stake."

> *Staking your plants is important for vegetables and flowers alike. Sometimes large showy flowers . . . can become quite top-heavy after a rain, so staking is a simple technique to keep them from sagging. And staking your vegetable plants is an effective way to ensure a bountiful harvest.*

> *Stakes are often forsaken at the expense of the flowers. Traditionally thought to be intrusive and unattractive... Carefully staked plants will show no visible support because the healthy and attractive foliage will hide the stakes... And staked plants are far more appealing than their unstaked counterparts who cannot hold their pretty flower heads up to please anyone.*

The best way to stake is to begin early in the growing sea-
son so you can easily train your plant and its subsequent
foliage... Staking mature plants whose foliage is flopping
is a far more difficult task, and the leaves and flowers are
not as appealing as if the plant were trained from the
start.

This is an amazing parallel to the process of "grow-ing" a new real estate sales business. Securing help in the beginning of your career yields hope for a bountiful, successful business. The garden stake is intended to support the large flower heads under the added pressure of rain and wind; in much the same way, an accountability system is in place to help an agent over a hump with a difficult client, through the rough spots of a tumultuous transaction, or around the obstacles that keep an agent from prospecting for new business. The self-defeating practice of forsaking plant stakes on the notion that they are unattractive is the same lens an agent looks through to only the expense of adding a coach or accountability partner to their business plan. In the same way that the healthy foliage eventually hides the stakes, an agent should instead consider the benefit of increased revenue that will make the cost worth its merit. Stakes act as an anchor to support a plant in its most delicate life phase ~ the beginning. The start of its life is the most vulnerable, because the strength of its early development determines its ability to withstand environmental pressures and be fruitful at harvest time. Similarly, the success of an agent's real estate business is developed in those critical initial months when the agent is either being trained and developed to thrive or neglected to fade away into the shadows of mediocrity.

There are various ways to engage the practice of accountability in your real estate career. I will present five in this chapter.

1. **One-on-one coaching.** You can employ a business coach or request the time of your managing broker for this method of accountability. One-on-one coaching gives you the benefits of individualized attention and business strategy tailored to your personal needs. In this individual setting, you and your coach can identify your inadequacies and create a business strategy that focuses on your strengths, to allow your true potential to be revealed.

2. **Group coaching.** Find out if your sponsoring broker offers this kind of training format for new licensees. If not, you can retain the services of a group-coaching program, which can be less costly than purchasing individual coaching services. A business coach or mentor agent usually leads these sessions, focusing on a different topic every week. A comprehensive group-coaching program will have topics ranging from negotiation and working with buyers to getting the listing and completing contracts. These programs resemble "on-the-job training," allowing you to learn as you grow your business. A group-coaching format also offers you the opportunity to learn from the successes and challenges of the other trainees. You become part of a group in an autonomous business environment where you could all too easily feel like you are very alone.

3. **Business networking and accountability groups.** If you cannot find an existing business networking group, it is fairly easy to create one. These groups are made up of businesses from different industries who get together periodically to exchange contacts and prospects, and to report the progress of their

business-building efforts. At the end of every session, each business should establish a goal that they are working toward, one that they will accomplish before the next session. Time is set aside at each session to review these goals, to make sure that they were accomplished by the business owner.

4. **Agent-peer accountability group.** This group can include agents from your office or from other offices. Members assemble weekly to perform productive activities like making calls to For Sale by Owners, expired listings or their marketing databases. During the calling breaks, agents record the number of appointments generated by each agent, creating healthy competition amongst the members of the group. Agents also exchange strategies, discussing what works and what does not work, and then discuss systems they have implemented that might help another agent.

5. **Employ an agent mentor.** Ask for help from a productive agent at your company. Ride along as they take buyers out for showings and go on listing presentations. In exchange for their mentoring, offer to do administrative tasks for the agent. This

will also help you when it is time to complete paperwork for your own clients. When you are working with your first few buyers or sellers, enlist the mentor agent's help, compensating the agent by sharing your commission on the transactions. This is a small cost to pay for training that will save you from making "rookie" errors that can be avoided by having an experienced agent guide you. As a rookie agent, partnering with a mentor agent also gives you credibility with potential buyers and sellers.

As you can see, there are various ways to engage the benefits of accountability in your business-building efforts. Try a few of these methods until you find the one that works best in propelling you forward. You may also find that one of them works better for a particular season of your career. For example, for some, individual coaching is most beneficial when they are in the start-up or expansion phase of their business, while group coaching works best when they are in an implementation phase. Whatever method you choose, you are ultimately choosing to be committed to growing a profitable business while being held accountable for reaching your dreams and goals.

CHAPTER 6

AFFILIATE PARTNERSHIPS:
COOPERATIVE HARVEST

"Two people are better off than one, for they can help each other
succeed." ~ Ecclesiastes 4:9

"When a group of individual minds are coordinated and function in
harmony, the increased energy created through that alliance becomes
available to every individual in the group." ~ Napoleon Hill

Have you ever seen geese flying in a V-formation? Ever wondered why they fly in that manner? Research has determined that the flapping of each bird's wings creates uplift for the bird directly behind it. This formation increases the speed and distance the flock is able to travel together, compared to each of them trying to go the distance alone. Likewise, rookie agents would be wise to create partnerships with affiliate businesses that can enhance their services and marketing programs, helping them get farther in less time.

The core affiliate businesses you need on your team are real estate attorneys, home inspectors, lenders, mortgage brokers, homeowner's insurance agents, home warranty companies, appraisers and (depending on what state you live in) title company representatives. Develop relationships with at least two or three individuals from each category, and always let the client make the final choice as to whom they prefer to do business with. Each of these businesses will be involved during a different part of the transaction.

The real estate attorney will legally advise the buyer or seller during the transaction, from the time of contract negotiation through the closing. A home inspector will inspect the home under contract, to ensure there are no property defects and mechanical system malfunctions. In the case that there are defects in the property, the attorney will negotiate concessions on behalf of the buyer.

Financial representatives offer financing vehicles that make it possible for a buyer to purchase a home. Lenders create financing alternatives from among the products available at their lending institution. Conversely, mortgage brokers review the products of various lending institutions to find the alternative that is most favorable for the buyer. Contact your financial representative before taking a buyer out on the first showing, to verify the price range that is appropriate for their budget. Once the buyer has a property under contract, the financial representative then proceeds with the underwriting process of the loan.

For most loan products, it is required that a buyer secure homeowner's insurance on the property before the closing of escrow; consequently, the homeowner's insurance representative is needed while the buyer's file is in its underwriting process at the bank. It is also a good idea for buyers to purchase a home warranty on a home, because it will cover the cost of repairs of the appliances and main systems of the house during the first twelve-to-eighteen months of ownership. (Newly constructed or converted properties typically come with a developer's warranty.) The time to ascertain a buyer's desire for home warranty coverage is while you are writing the contract or offer to purchase. The actual purchase of the warranty takes place at the closing table. Frequently, the seller will purchase this warranty coverage for the buyer. This coverage can also be purchased for the seller, to cover the home while it is an active listing.

In a situation where you have an all-equity buyer who is paying cash or using personal financing methods, an appraiser becomes necessary to certify the value of the property, after the contract is signed and before the closing takes place. If a buyer is using traditional financing, the bank typically uses its own appraiser to determine objective property value. In some situations, a seller may want to verify the value of their home before putting it on the market. If you live in a state where real estate agents also handle title work for the client, a title company representative is contacted to order a title report and verify no clouds or imperfections in the title as well as to secure title insurance for the buyer; this takes place after you have an executed contract.

There are a number of reasons why it is important to build these professional relationships with affiliate businesses. Following are 10 reasons why these relationships are crucial to the building of your business.

1. **Referrals, referrals, referrals.** Your network and marketing database expands every time you meet new people. Exchanging contacts with another business also increases your database. Sharing cus-

tomers allows both businesses to benefit by expanding their reach.

2. **No selling.** When a client is referred to you by another vendor, there is typically no need to sell yourself to the client. Most of the work has been done by the referring affiliate; the client trusts the word of the one who referred them.

3. **Joint bank account.** A combined marketing budget allows you to reach more prospects; again, joint ventures expand your marketing reach.

4. **Who are you?** Being sponsored and supported by an established name in the real estate industry enhances your credibility. If you have sponsors and affiliate partners, it implies that you are an experienced agent with established contacts.

5. **Synergy.** The synergy of two businesses reaching for common goals motivates both owners, and each becomes a source of accountability for the other.

6. **Satisfaction guaranteed.** Clients benefit by not having to choose necessary vendors based on trial and error. Having previously established these relationships with your affiliates, you know the quality of service being delivered. The work ethic, service

excellence, reliability, and integrity of these affiliates match that of your business. This increases your value in the eyes of the consumer.

7. **One-stop shop.** Your clientele will appreciate the fact that you have all the professional resources they need for buying or selling their home. They need only contact you; you then become the main point of reference for any real-estate-related need they encounter. When you establish yourself in this manner, it keeps your clients needing and calling you, even after their transaction has closed.

8. **Discounts.** Who does not like saving money on a product or service? Establish coupon and discount programs with your affiliate partners that you can then offer to your clients when they use those services. This benefit for your clientele is another great reason for them to work with you.

9. **Revolving door.** It can be difficult to continuously work with the new practitioners that every client brings to the table. An established relationship with an affiliate lends itself to systems and familiarity that help you move efficiently through a transaction. You are confident that they are competent

and that you won't have to do their job. You create ebb and flow for follow-up, follow-through, information exchange and handling bottlenecks in a transaction.

10. **Star treatment.** As the relationships develop, your affiliates give preferential treatment to your clients, knowing that there is more to come if they continue to exceed the expectations of your clients.

The following are a few bonus tips for working with affiliate partners:

Develop a client satisfaction survey that measures the quality of service received by your clients from your affiliates. Your client will complete the survey after the close of the transaction. Share this complimentary market research with your affiliate partners on a quarterly basis. It is a benefit to both you and your affiliates; it helps them improve their services and lets you know how your clients are being treated.

As your business develops, create a vendor directory and allow affiliates to purchase ad space in the directory. Or barter marketing services by supplying advertising space in the directory in exchange for the vendor paying for a mailing to your database, or for real estate seminar advertising. The directory can then be distributed in various ways. It can be given to your buyers and sellers in their information packet at the initial client meeting. Co-agents are always looking for vendor referrals; you can make the directory available to all agents at your real estate office. The directory should be updated annually and can be mailed out to your marketing database as one of your "touches" for the year. You can also add other businesses to the directory that are real-estate-related disciplines, such as remodeling contractors, home furnishing stores, interior decorators, home appliance outlets, window treatment specialty stores, professional movers, van and truck rental companies, painters, carpet installers, cookware specialty companies, California closet stores, etc. Advertising dollars generated from this directory can then be used for your business marketing budget.

It may take time to create a dream team that fits with you and your business style. But be patient with the process because creating a team of affiliates can work to your advantage in a myriad of ways.

CHAPTER 7

MONEY MANAGEMENT:
FROM THE FIELDS TO THE MARKET

"The man who had received the five talents went at once and put his money to work and gained five more." – Matthew 25:16

"He who owns a hundred sheep must fight with fifty wolves."
~ Plutarchus

Thus far, you have established goals and learned how to manage your time to create more productive days as a new real estate licensee. This book has also equipped you with inspiring thoughts to help you persevere during the difficult days, and has offered direction to fine-tune your marketing focus. You have also learned the value of including others in the process, to support you as you build your business. As you grow your successful business, you will ultimately begin to reap financial gain from your sales transactions. This chapter offers some basic strategies for managing the revenue from your sales.

First, there needs to be a transitional shift in the way you think about income, now that you are an independent contractor. According to Webster's Dictionary, an independent contractor is "one that contracts to do work or perform a service for another but retains total and free control over the means or methods used in doing the work or performing the service." By contrast, Webster's Dictionary defines an employee as "a person usually below the executive level who is hired by another to perform a service especially for wages or salary and is under the other's control." Therein lies the shift. You do not get paid for showing up at the office, surfing the internet or going to lunch with your favorite co-agents. You will now receive 100% commission income based solely on <u>results</u>. Your payroll and income taxes will no longer be paid for you from your checks. You are now responsible for making tax payments directly to the Internal Revenue Service. Two weeks' worth of service no longer means receiving a paycheck on the second Friday. As an independent contractor, a check usually comes in eight-to-ten weeks ~ or more ~ after you begin working with a client.

This chapter is meant to speak to the individual who enters the real estate industry as an independent contractor agent, not as an employee. As you can see from the definition, the difference lies in who manages the time and methods of the agent. Because you are in full control of your time, money and methods as an independent contractor, it is necessary for you to put plans in place to structure and manage your finances. Following are five tips that can help you structure a basic financial plan for success.

1. Create your own deductions from every check. Pay yourself first by creating a deduction for personal savings; allocate 5-10% of each check for savings. A deduction for payroll taxes should be allocated next. Seek the advice of an accountant to determine the appropriate percentage that should be deducted from each check. Marketing/business development budgets should account for 8-10% or more of each check, as well. Depending on your financial stability, you may also want to allocate a percentage of each check for a vacation budget. Many times, life

gets busy and we don't make time to take care of and restore ourselves. If you have funds set aside for this purpose, it becomes a little easier to make time for rest and relaxation. (If you are not financially in a place to establish a vacation fund at this time, make it a goal to get there.)

2. Set up a separate bank account for each of these deductions, to deter commingling of funds. This will also keep you from using another account's funds for personal expenses. When you receive a commission check, make a deposit into each account, based upon its predetermined allocation percentage.

3. Quarterly tax payments need to be made directly to the Internal Revenue Service. These payments will be made from the bank account you establish for payroll taxes. This is very important! Many agents who haven't planned ahead have to resort to using savings accounts or personal credit at tax time to pay their tax bill. Or worse, they receive IRS liens on personal property or levies on bank accounts for the amount of the tax debt. Also, be aware that IRS

fines are assessed when you don't make the estimated quarterly tax payments.

4. Determine what your personal monthly expenses are. Establish a savings goal of at least 6 months' worth of living expenses in a liquid account like a Certificate of Deposit (CD), high-yield savings account or money market account. Real estate agents who have this financial cushion do not feel the temptation to push a deal through that is not in the best interest of their client, just in order to get paid sooner.

5. My final piece of advice is to get a financial planner. As an independent contractor, you don't have a company 401K plan, health insurance plan, or pension. Consequently, it is in your best interest to seek the advice of a financial planner who can help structure a comprehensive financial plan that will address these needs.

Implementing these simple, but key, financial strategies will go a long way toward setting you up for wealth and prosperity as your business grows.

CHAPTER 8

FIT TO RUN A BUSINESS:
TILL THE SOIL

"But you have made me as strong as a wild bull..." ~ Psalm 92:10

"Strength comes by exercise; activity is the very condition of life."
– E.G. White

Health and fitness play a role in the success of many entrepreneurs and high-power executives. These highly successful individuals have developed systems and patterns that consistently move them to higher levels, perhaps because "[success] lies in the daily disciplines of a champion," according to Dirk Zeller. Consequently, many people are interested in learning how such busy people can find the time to work out. For this chapter of the book, I interviewed my own personal trainer and running coach, LaVerne Young of 4Ever Young Fitness in Chicago, IL, about the effect that health and fitness have on the success of so many. Our conversation follows, with Young's responses in italics.

First of all, let's talk about why fitness is so important. . . .

It is a way of life. I tell myself and my clients, 'every day you have to work out like your life depends on it, because it does. If you don't take care of your house, you won't have anywhere to live.'

That is so simple, yet so profound. So, following that thought pattern, tell me what role health and fitness play in one's ultimate success.

Health and fitness regimens instill a spirit of commitment. For instance, to train for a marathon, you commit to running 5 days a week, increasing mileage every week, denying yourself most food indulgences, preparing your body and wrapping your mind around 26.2 miles. It transcends into every aspect of your life. Consequently, you become more disciplined, focused and committed in all areas of your life. Some secrets are revealed to you; you begin to discover a new you every day.

As an entrepreneur, it is easy to become overwhelmed by the many responsibilities and opportunities of each day. How do you make exercise fit into such a busy schedule?

Health and fitness are first priority on every hand. It is how you face the day.

That makes sense because the ability to prioritize is a tool that successful people use every day. Exercise must first become a priority; then sacrifices will be made, where necessary, to carve out exercise time in your schedule. First thing in the morning works best for many because it is the *"no excuses"* time of the day. Before 6:00 a.m., there aren't many distractions that can get in your way.

The world has entered a health and fitness craze. Countless commercials, infomercials and magazine ads claim they have the latest and greatest exercise program. How do you choose one?

Choose what is practical and that which you can do for the rest of your life. Any exercise program will work. The question is, how long will it work for you? You have to select diets and exercise programs that will last a lifetime. There are no quick fixes and no magic pills, only hard work and lots of it. If it were as easy as a pill, you would have no fat millionaires.

Do you have to work with a personal trainer? Why not just go to the gym and work out alone?

Thanks for asking this question! Though I am a personal trainer, I also have a personal trainer. It is imperative for people that are looking for optimum results to seek advice, wise counsel, and direction from a certified professional. Most women planning their wedding will not do their own hair and nails, nor make their own dress. We hire professionals for various services because we trust the knowledge and experience of the professional and want the best results possible. However, when it comes to our bodies, we go buy a magazine that has a circulation of 10,000 and tear out a workout and diet plan, expecting it be a tailored fit to our needs! A certified personal trainer/coach is important for the optimum results which can be obtained through a customized and result-specific program and regimen.

I want to address some common questions and concerns that people have about exercising. How do you respond to someone who says, "I am young. Why do I need to exercise?"

For the same reason a Mercedes Benz needs a tune up . . . maintenance! 85% of life is maintenance. Once you obtain something in life, you have to work to keep it. Start with the end in mind. Women that reach middle age maintaining a fit look and healthy weight normally started exercising at a young age. And, of course, the reverse is true for out-of-shape women. Unfit middle-

aged women typically did not make exercise and sports a part of their young lifestyle. In addition, heart disease can start as early as the tender age of thirteen.

That is an amazing fact. What about the person who says, "I am middle-aged, I take my medication, and I feed my body well. Why do I need to exercise?"

Why exercise? Because that is what the doctor told you anyway, when you started taking medication. Every doctor orders that you comply with your medication guidelines, eat right and exercise. Exercise does the body good!

I have heard some people proclaim, "My knees are bad, so I can't exercise!"

Your knees are bad!? You can't exercise!? No, if your knees are bad, you can't afford not to exercise. These individuals should be exercising; it will help maintain whatever healthy part of their knee is remaining. Aqua exercise is great for not-so-healthy knees.

And what about the one who says, "I do Tae Bo at home, when I have time. Does that count?"

Yes, all calories burned are points toward fitness earned. It doesn't matter what you do and where, it just matters that you get your body moving.

That reminds me of the definition of momentum; objects in motion stay in motion, while objects at rest stay at rest. Getting your body moving towards one goal will give you the momentum you need to get it going in other areas of your life, as well.

I know of a couple of top producers that compete in triathlons. How do you think that plays a part in their success?

Exercise fosters and instills in an individual a greater level of confidence. It allows one to break through to the other side, to go beyond thresholds and break out of comfort zones. It dispels a lot of fear. Again, the benefits transcend into every facet of our lives.

I wholeheartedly agree with that. Running my first two marathons caused the transformation of my mindset. After completing the Chicago marathon, I immediately thought it was a fluke; there was no possible way that I really traveled 26.2 miles *on foot!* My condescending thought patterns began to echo loudly that the excitement and adrenaline rush of the event, among other nonsense explanations, were the only reasons I made it to the finish line. Strange as it seems, my mind had a very difficult time wrapping itself around the idea that I had accomplished this amazing feat, even though I had the blistered toes, sore muscles and medal to prove it. In an effort to resolve this cognitive dissonance, I continued my training through

Chicago's winter and, two months later, ran the Honolulu marathon ~ just to make sure I could really do it. Consequently, one of the secrets revealed to me was the power of the mind to cause belief in false realties about one's great potential and abilities. I now believe that I can achieve anything my imagination dares to dream. The fact that I am right now penning my first manuscript is a testament to that fact.

So the question that remains is how to get started on a health and fitness regimen. What tips can you suggest for making this lifestyle change?

The best way to implement any change in your life is to get some form of accountability structure in place, to ensure that you are reaching your goals and functioning at your greatest potential. Exercise groups, exercise classes, and one-on-one personal training can all help you achieve that goal on different levels.

Experience has taught me that I can go farther when I live a balanced life – making sure that I take care of my physical self, as well as my professional self.

CHAPTER 9

SUCCESS SECRETS FROM
TOP PRODUCERS:
TALES OF THE FARMER NEXT DOOR

"Work hard and become a leader" ~ *Proverbs 12:24*

"The successful warrior is the average man, with laser-like focus."
~ *Bruce Lee*

I interviewed four trailblazers in the industry, to get the inside scoop on what they did to become successful and maintain success. Through their stories, you will also discover their inadequacies and challenges. In addition, these profiles will identify the people in their lives that contributed to their success. It is my desire that you hear your thoughts and see your own reality in their stories; in so doing, you will realize that their story can be your story as well.

Michael DiPasquale

www.mdipasquale.com

2007 Realtor Magazine's "30 Under 30" Award

3rd year in the business

Average Sales Volume: $5.3 million

Main source of business: Referrals

Real Estate One, South Lyon, MI

Salesperson

"We are in the business of lead generation. The rest is just details."

Fear was the main factor that contributed to Mike's successful transition from rookie agent to veteran agent. When Mike was a mere 22 years old, he was laid off from his sales management position, after he had recently purchased a home. As fate would have it, he had been studying for the real estate exam and thus was able to get his license and start to build his business, soon thereafter. For Mike, not knowing the source of his next mortgage payment drove him to success. Desperation has a way of making you do things you would not otherwise do without lots of coaxing. When faced with the <u>need</u> to succeed, only restless abandon and focused commitment to your goal will set you free.

For this young lad, his age was a perceived barrier to his rise in the industry. Mike was nervous that people would not trust his real estate knowledge because he was so young. He was so convinced of this that he used to tell himself, "If only I were 40, my sales production could be higher." Over time, and through experience, Mike developed more confidence in his abilities, and his age was no longer an obstacle to keep him from his goals. Notice that I used the phrase "perceived barrier" because, although Mike is still relatively very young, he is now a trailblazer in the industry.

One false impression about success that Mike would like to dispel is the misconception that life is easier once you are running a successful real estate business. According to Mike, "my life was 100 times easier when I was broke." He no longer worries about the mortgage payment but now tosses and turns at night, thinking about business-related concerns. The lesson that Mike has learned is, "There are no shortcuts to success. Nothing happens fast. It is all building blocks." For him, however, it is all worth it because he sees his hard work paying off.

Mike faces reality about being a real estate agent. "We are in the business of lead generation; the rest is just details." The well-known activities of the business, like showing property, writing contracts and securing lockboxes, are a mere 15-20% of his business activity. To remind him of that fact daily, the sign on his computer reads, "Your only business is lead generation." Mike makes it a point to stay focused on revenue-generating activities, and away from things that consume his time with no financial benefit during the work day.

Staying on-time and on-schedule can be a challenge to a busy real estate agent. But on a day-to-day basis, in the absence of an assistant, Mike uses his PDA/phone combo and laptop to keep him on top of To Do lists, appointments, and prospecting with his contact-management database.

Mike has benefited from various coaching styles during his rise to the top, utilizing individual and group coaching programs, as well as extensive classroom-style trainings. Mike's business coach proved not to be the fast-talking salesman type but, rather, genuinely cared about his personal and business success. Therefore, he made a huge impact on Mike's business.

Being at the pinnacle of success in his life, right now, Mike gives the credit to his aforementioned business coach, to his managing broker who believed in him from the very beginning, and to the loan officer with whom he has developed an affiliate relationship that has grown to be his marketing and accountability partner.

NINA CHEN

www.ninachen.net

2006 Finalist-Real Estate Apprentice Rookie Award

1½ years in the business

Average Sales Volume: $2 million

Main source of business: Postcard mailings

Re/Max Centre Realty, State College, PA

Salesperson

"Remember who you are representing. Don't focus on the outcome;

focus on the client's best interest."

For this newly degreed Bachelor of Fine Arts in Ceramics graduate, guidance and training from her mentor agent is one of the greatest factors that has contributed to her success. Nina's mentor agent walked her through her initial transactions, step by step, helping her to remember all the pieces she had to juggle. By partnering with a mentor agent, she also convinced her clients that the transactions would be skillfully handled, with an experienced agent guiding Nina. Her first two transactions, generated through her sphere of influence, gave Nina "that boost of confidence to say I could do this." Becoming a finalist for the 2006 Real Estate Apprentice Rookie Award also inspired Nina with the confidence that she needed to persist through the rough times in the beginning. Confidence-building is a seed that has grown success in Nina's real estate practice.

But success does not come easy, according to Nina. Living in today's "instant gratification" society, many people desire immediate success, perceiving that "you get a license and then money just comes at you," says Nina. But real estate sales are not that easy. You have to do the work of establishing yourself in your market before you can reap the benefit.

Nina has identified a couple of personal challenges that could potentially stand in the way of her success. "Staying self-motivated and doing what I say I am going to do," are personal development skills that she works to improve upon, every day. For Nina, staying focused on the positives in business instead of the negatives helps keep her motivated and on-track.

Nina is also a member of a peer accountability group. This group of professionals meets biweekly, spanning different industries but sharing one commonality...they are all newbies in their respective careers. The sense of sharing a similar challenge with a group of people produces camaraderie, support, encouragement, and ideas for combating common struggles.

Nina employs a systematic prospecting plan to keep her business out of the "cyclical income" cycle and in a continuous flow. Her marketing plan includes a biweekly real-estate-related email newsletter that is distributed to the 200 contacts in her database. Her 200 contacts are a combination of friends, family, floor-call prospects and open-house guests. Her prospecting plan also includes mailing 1000 "Just Listed" and "Just Sold" postcards regularly to targeted neighborhoods. There is an email address on the card that recipients can use to get more details about a property. This allows Nina to capture email addresses and make them part of her biweekly email marketing campaign. Nina also tracks her leads so that she can ascertain where to best spend her marketing dollars.

Characteristics of an entrepreneur include the ability to make tough decisions and take risks. Three months into her sales career, Nina had to make just such a tough decision. It had become a struggle to work her part-time job and still give focused attention to her clients and new business. The odds were against Nina; the business field itself was completely new to this Fine Arts major, she was not financially stable, and she was spending money on training and seminars to gain the knowledge she knew she needed to become successful. Not wanting to leave her steady income, she nevertheless "took a leap of faith and left the part-time job," in spite of her fear. This risk paid off for Nina, as she remained sufficiently focused and committed to her goal to attain success in the business.

Nina didn't rise to the top alone. She is grateful for her personal mentor, who helped her to figure out her dreams and the roads to follow to reach them. She also could not have done it without the training help of her mentor agent, and the supportive role her parents played as she pursued a career path that is non-traditional in her family.

Bertina M. Power

www.yourpowerbroker.com

Several appearances on HGTV programming in:

"Designed to Sell," "My House is Worth WHAT?" and

"National Open House"

5 years in the business

Average Sales Volume: $6.5 million

Main source of business: Email marketing/Referrals

Keller Williams Premier Power Brokers, Chicago, IL

Operating Principal/Broker

"Just like you have to water the grass to make it grow, you've got to feed your database daily if you want it to produce sales and referrals."

If you are a full-time agent, you wake up unemployed every day, so you have to have passion," says Bertina, and passionate she is about the business of relational marketing and real estate sales. For Bertina, real estate is all about creating relationships and keeping in touch. She is able to stay in touch by using a contact-management database software system. This system allows her to keep names, phone numbers, email addresses, notes from previous conversations, birthdays and other pertinent information all in one place. Bertina says everybody goes in her database: past and prospective clients, open-house guests, and people she meets at the post office or grocery store. Once they are in her database, she is able to systematically communicate with them, based on the category she places them in. Through quarterly or monthly emails, phone calls and snail mail, she is able to "touch" her database regularly throughout the year. With every communication, prospects and potential referral sources are reminded that Bertina is still actively working in the business and is ready to serve their real estate needs. This system allows Bertina to streamline the flow of her transactions and stay away from cyclical income.

One of the secrets to her success is that she captures and engages both present and future clients. She is careful to stay fresh in the minds of people not looking to buy or sell right now, by adding them to her database, sending emails and making periodic phone calls. Bertina sees these future potential buyers and sellers as missed opportunities for most agents, rookie and experienced alike. In this business, you have to continually keep future business on your radar. When you think about your financial stability, you have to ask yourself what deals or clients you have in the pipeline for future revenue. The opportunity to make money today is already gone. Realize that any deals you are doing right now are the result of work you did sometime in the past. Bertina puts it this way: "You must do something today to ensure you will get a check in the near future."

Today, she advises that rookie agents set aside at least 3 hours a day for prospecting, whether business is flowing or stagnant, but that was one of Bertina's greatest challenges as a new licensee. Instead of exercising a daily commitment to her business, she found herself building her daily routine based on emotion. On the days she did not *feel* like working, she did not; and when she felt energized and ready to go, she went full-throttle. But she soon realized that she was taking her income on that emotional roller coaster ride with her.

That is precisely one of the misconceptions she thinks people buy into about this business: that free time abounds for the real estate agent. But Bertina retorts, "Successful agents are not the ones sleeping until 12 o'clock. They are up answering phones and making calls by 9:00 a.m., as if they were getting paid to be there." Bertina says it was necessary for her to "put in the time, to get out what I wanted from my business."

As she made these realizations and gained momentum in her business, her broker at the time made an observation about the way she interacted with clients. He mentioned that she oversold customers, talking more than she listened. Bertina learned to be more conscientious in her client conversations by listening more to the needs of the client. In essence, this allowed her to service the needs of the client better, because she better understood what they were. Although she had to learn to tame her conversation with clients, it is that very gift for gab that has landed her roles on several real-estate reality shows on HGTV, including the popular, "Designed to Sell."

Having realized great success in her real estate career in a short amount of time, Bertina recognizes that she could not have attained such success on her own. This success includes ownership of the first African-American-owned Keller Williams Realty franchise in her region. She believes that, from the beginning, her mother prepared her for where she now stands in the limelight of success, always encouraging her to be a lifelong learner. Thus, she knows how to take a lesson from both the positive and the nega-

tive influences in the real estate industry. She acknowl-
edges that she has come across "some in the industry that
teach you how you do not want to run your business." Her
spirituality and her husband are also a major part of her
support system, keeping her grounded and in balance in the
midst of such success.

JANICE CORLEY-BLANEY

www.sudlersothebysrealty.com

Featured in <u>Ebony Magazine</u>, March 2005

Who's Who: Influential Black Chicagoan list

Numerous High Sales Volume awards

19 years in the business

Average Sales Volume: $450 million

Main source of business: Networking

Sudler Sotheby's International Realty, Chicago, IL

CEO/President

"If you are disciplined, you will do very, very well, not average, but very well."

For Janice Corley-Blaney a veteran powerbroker in the real estate industry, the success formula is very simple. "You need two ingredients in order to sell real estate . . . a buyer and a seller." Janice believes in keeping it simple all around. She even returns her own phone messages and schedules her own appointments. Janice believes getting into this business can be relatively inexpensive if an agent keeps it on the basic level of being "primarily focused on [bringing together] a buyer and a seller." She believes in Dale Carnegie's "KISS" phrase: "<u>K</u>eep <u>I</u>t <u>S</u>imple, <u>S</u>tupid."

But Janice primarily attributes her success to another essential business component: discipline. In leading her team of real estate agents, she notices that "agents do exceptionally well if they treat themselves as if they are working for someone and not just look at their watch in the middle of the day and go get a manicure, because you couldn't do that if you worked for someone." Creating a system and structure for her days gives her a time and place to be doing something productive, to generate new business, attract new agents to her brokerage or transact her own real estate dealings.

Janice has scaled the ladder of success, feeling there is no great challenge or obstacle that has stood in her way because she has no competition. It is her mindset that she has no need to compete with anyone else because we are all made differently, with a unique purpose and definition of success. Consequently, there is no one in the entire world that is her competition. In her eyes, "I am my own worst enemy." However, she has noticed a common obstacle to success amongst new sales agents. She recognizes that there are some who struggle to reach the next level because "they have a mindset that they have not conditioned, feeling like they don't *deserve* to go to the next level." It is necessary for these agents to change their attitude or mindset about success so that they can achieve it.

If an agent were to ask Janice for a plan to streamline the income of their real estate sales business, in keeping with her aura of simplicity, she would give this simple solution: "Write a schedule; go into the office, consistently sticking to the schedule on a daily basis; make your prospecting calls [or do your prospecting activities] to produce 4-6 appointments per week, and you will never have to worry about a 'down' market, because you will always be working on developing new business." She goes on to warn, "When agents get busy, they quit prospecting for new business, and when you quit prospecting, you are on your way out of business."

For her schedule and day-to-day affairs, Janice relies only on her Blackberry. She does not get carried away with all the gadgets and newest software being sold to real estate practitioners. She practices "KISS" and uses the daily newspaper, For Sale signs and Broker Open Houses to study her market and stay in the know about its agents and properties.

Janice has had several mentors and coaches, over the years, to propel her to the top. When she first got into the business, she employed a coach whom she "respected because of her ability to run several real estate offices with many agents that loved her." In addition to other real estate coaches along the way, Janice also chooses local business persons as mentors, based on their general business acumen. These experiences have played a role in her stellar achievements.

Being that there is always a cost for making great strides in any industry, one of the major risks Janice took was to purchase her first real estate company on "blind faith," as she calls it. A newly divorced single parent with two children, she had a stable sales management job at a major real estate firm, but Janice decided the moment was right to start her own real estate company. "Blind faith" and belief in herself outweighed the risk of leveraging her home to make the purchase. That was seven years ago. Since paying off that loan, she has grown her company through mergers and acquisitions, never having to leverage her home again. Instead of thinking "what if," she thought, "I have faith and a strong belief in myself and what I feel like I can do."

These superstar agents have some other words of wisdom to share with those entering the real estate industry. Michael Dipasquale advises that new licensees should "be adaptable to the home sales environment." Changing markets during his short time in the business have caused him to transition from the first-time home buyer market to the foreclosure market. Nina sees the silver lining in the clouds when considering the state of the current real estate market across the nation. She offers, "Though it is challenging, being able to succeed in a down market really sharpens you for later on." Bertina suggests that new agents have "a little knowledge about all the pieces that put this real estate pie together." For example, she considers it advantageous to go on home inspections with your clients, to learn how to distinguish between major and minor issues when you are showing a client property. Janice Corley advises that agents study and know their chosen market intimately, because "Knowledge is key."

This book has shared a lot of information and inspiration with you. My final hope for you is that you don't get bogged down with trying to do it all the *right way*. Instead, just get started. Experience has taught me that in building something, there is much trial and error in the process. If you become comfortable with the fact that you may not get it right the first time, but have the audacity to try again, you understand what it means to strive for success ~ a success that is not measured by comparing yourself to another but, rather, one that looks at your unique gifts and talents, and challenges you to be excellent.

"Excellence is striving to accomplish my personal best, within the limited circumstances and resources with which I have to work and to be willing to accept the limitations of my human talents. I can never control my environment nor the abilities and weaknesses of those with whom I work. Therefore, I will do my best with what I have and be satisfied."–Unknown

Perfection can never be attained. Excellence is the true goal.

I s your new real estate sales business suffering from any of the following challenges?

- Roller-coaster income...

- Insufficient closings and clients...

- Licensed some time ago with no closings to date?

- Cold-calling efforts not producing clients?

- No affiliate partnerships to strengthen credibility?

- Working 24/7 with no time for family or self?

- Insufficient marketing dollars. . .

- Lack of negotiation skills and strategies...

- No marketing materials to attract buyers and sellers?

- Lack of customer service skills to generate repeat referrals?

- Lack of business accountability to reach goals?

To obtain assistance or direction in implementing foundational tools to grow your real estate sales business, please visit us online at:

www.RookieAgentBootCamp.com

Or contact us at:

info@rookieagentbootcamp.com

Ramelia – once a successful rookie real estate agent, now a dynamic rookie agent business coach – is the Founder and Director of Rookie Agent Boot Camp. She uses various foundational tools and success strategies to motivate new licensees to reach their full potential and achieve work/life balance. As a rookie agent, she appeared on the cover of the national "Realtor Magazine" as one of the nation's "30 under 30" real estate agents to watch in June of 2004. She was also quoted and profiled in "Prudential Leader" magazine that year. Ramelia credits coaching and accountability for her success as a real estate agent, and she desires to give that back to the real estate community. She has also reached "Expert Author" status for her rookie-agent-focused articles featured on www.EzineArticles.com. She is a licensed Broker/Owner in the state of Illinois.

ABOUT ROOKIE AGENT BOOT CAMP

Rookie Agent Boot Camp is a 7-month real estate agent training and development program for new licensees. This program was designed to decrease the learning curve and thus the amount of time it takes new agents to generate their first 4-5 transactions. When agents can generate transactions in those initial critical months, they are prepared to reach their highest potential in the real estate sales business. This unique program offers both group and one-on-one coaching. Rookie Agent Boot Camp increases the possibility of success for new real estate licensees.

www.ingramcontent.com/pod-product-compliance
Lightning Source LLC
Chambersburg PA
CBHW022108210326
41521CB00029B/318